RECKLESS LOVE

Leader Guide

Reckless Love
Jesus' Call to Love Our Neighbor

Reckless Love
978-1-5018-7986-9
978-1-5018-7987-6 eBook

Reckless Love DVD
978-1-5018-7990-6

Reckless Love Leader Guide
978-1-5018-7988-3
978-1-5018-7989-0 eBook

Also by Tom Berlin

6 Decisions That Will Change Your Life

6 Things We Should Know About God

6 Ways We Encounter God

Bearing Fruit

Defying Gravity

The Generous Church

High Yield

Overflow

Restored

TOM BERLIN

RECKLESS LOVE

JESUS' CALL TO
LOVE OUR NEIGHBOR

Leader Guide
By Mike S. Poteet

Abingdon Press / Nashville

RECKLESS LOVE
JESUS' CALL TO LOVE OUR NEIGHBOR
LEADER GUIDE

Copyright © 2019 Abingdon Press
All rights reserved.

978-1-5018-7988-3

19 20 21 22 23 24 25 26 27 28 — 10 9 8 7 6 5 4 3 2 1
MANUFACTURED IN THE UNITED STATES OF AMERICA

CONTENTS

INTRODUCTION

In *Reckless Love*, the Rev. Tom Berlin challenges readers to consider, extensively and at a personal level, how radical the biblical command to love God and to love our neighbor really is.

Deeply rooted in Hebrew Scripture and cited by Jesus in the New Testament as "the Great Commandment," the directive to love God and neighbor may sound simple on its surface. But any amount of time spent reflecting on it reveals its complexity. *How* do we love God and neighbor? *Who* is the neighbor we are to love? Can love be commanded at all?

Reckless Love touches on these questions and many more, but never shies away from the conviction that the life of love God commands is, in fact, the life God created all human beings to live. Pursuing it is worth any discomfort, any confusion, any cost. This life of love transforms us into the people we were always meant to be.

This six-session study guide gives small group leaders a resource they can use to spur their own reflections on *Reckless Love* and to guide discussions of its content in adult Christian education settings.

The six sessions directly correspond to the six chapters in *Reckless Love*.

- **Session 1: Begin with Love**
- What does the Great Commandment actually call us to do? Participants will explore the concept of love and take practical steps toward beginning their days and encounters in loving ways.

7

- **Session 2: Expand the Circle**
- Who is the neighbor God commands us to love? Participants will take a close look at their "relational circles" and consider how they need to expand those networks in order to fulfill the Great Commandment.

- **Session 3: Lavish Love**
- What does God's love look like on a day-to-day basis? Participants will look for answers in Jesus' "Sermon on the Plain" and will commit themselves to small but significant acts of love.

- **Session 4: Openhearted Love**
- What social barriers too often keep us from loving our neighbors? Participants will challenge social ideas about gender and race that contradict God's call to a radically inclusive love.

- **Session 5: Value the Vulnerable**
- Are there any "outsiders" where God's love is concerned? Participants will confront religious people's tendency to divide the world into "us" and "them," and will examine specific groups of vulnerable people whom Jesus engaged, as well as those groups' modern counterparts.

- **Session 6: Emulate Christ**
- How do we continue to grow in love? Participants will think about what it means to emulate Jesus and will look ahead to the transformation his command to love can bring.

Each session contains the following elements:

- **Session Goals:** Feel free to choose the goals you and your group deem most relevant, or touch on them all in your time together.

- **Biblical Foundations:** The key Scripture passages discussed in each chapter of *Reckless Love*, presented here in the New Revised

- Standard Version translation.

- **Chapter Summaries:** Not intended to replace the text, but to present important points in a concise format leaders and participants can review and refer to during each session.

- **Materials You Will Need:** No session requires elaborate or hard-to-find materials, but these lists will help you organize the simple supplies you will want. Many are optional, ensuring the study can be used in a variety of church or home settings.

- **Opening and Closing Activities:** These activities are usually, though not always, discussion-based, and help introduce or summarize the themes of each session.

- **Opening and Closing Prayers:** Leaders may read these prayers aloud verbatim or use them as models for their own prayers.

- **Video Presentation:** The 10- to 12-minute video presentation gives space for discussion and flows into the book conversation.

- **Book Discussion:** Questions designed to provoke discussion of *Reckless Love*, often quoting directly from the text.

- **Bible Study:** Use some or all of these questions to dig deeper into the Biblical Foundations of each session.

- **Extra Activity:** An optional activity described at the end of each session may be added if time allows.

May your group's study of *Reckless Love* empower you to love God and your neighbor more boldly and faithfully than ever before!

SESSION 1
BEGIN WITH LOVE

PLANNING THE SESSION

Session Goals

The conversations and activities in this session will equip participants to:

- Articulate their own biblically informed definitions of love and contrast these definitions with culturally prevalent definitions of love.
- Reflect on the ways love for God and love for neighbor intersect with and influence each other, and contribute to our continuing transformation into the people God wants us to be.
- Explore the tension in Christian life between committing ourselves to lives of love and depending upon God's love and grace.
- Plan to begin each day, encounter, conversation, and action with love.

Biblical Foundations

[28]One of the scribes came near and heard them disputing with one another, and seeing that he answered them well, he asked him, "Which commandment is the first of all?" [29]Jesus answered, "The first is, 'Hear, O Israel: the Lord our God, the Lord is one; [30]you shall love the Lord your God with all your heart, and with all your soul, and with all your mind, and with all your strength.' [31]The second is this, 'You shall love your neighbor as yourself.' There is no other commandment greater than these." [32]Then the scribe said to him, "You are right, Teacher; you have truly said that 'he is one, and besides him there is no other'; [33]and 'to love him with all the heart, and with all the understanding, and with all the strength,' and 'to love one's neighbor as oneself,'—this is much more important than all whole burnt offerings and sacrifices." [34]When Jesus saw that he answered wisely, he said to him, "You are not far from the kingdom of God." After that no one dared to ask him any question.

Mark 12:28-34

[16]Live by the Spirit, I say, and do not gratify the desires of the flesh. [17]For what the flesh desires is opposed to the Spirit, and what the Spirit desires is opposed to the flesh; for these are opposed to each other, to prevent you from doing what you want. [18]But if you are led by the Spirit, you are not subject to the law. [19]Now the works of the flesh are obvious: fornication, impurity, licentiousness, [20]idolatry, sorcery, enmities, strife, jealousy, anger, quarrels, dissensions, factions, [21]envy, drunkenness, carousing, and things like these. I am warning you, as I warned you before: those who do such things will not inherit the kingdom of God.

²²By contrast, the fruit of the Spirit is love, joy, peace, patience, kindness, generosity, faithfulness, ²³gentleness, and self-control. There is no law against such things. ²⁴And those who belong to Christ Jesus have crucified the flesh with its passions and desires. ²⁵If we live by the Spirit, let us also be guided by the Spirit. ²⁶Let us not become conceited, competing against one another, envying one another.

Galatians 5:16-26

Chapter Summary

In chapter 1, Tom Berlin identifies loving God as the most important goal of faithful living—as it was for ancient Israel, as it was for Jesus. God gave Israel the Law as the guide for demonstrating its love for God. But as Jesus said when summarizing the Law, we cannot truly or fully love God without loving our neighbor. And loving our neighbor, Berlin says, can be "a tall order."

While Christians sometimes think loving God will naturally lead to an overflowing love for our neighbors, Berlin suggests the reverse is also true, and arguably even more so: "It is only when we commit to love our neighbor and intentionally accomplish this goal that we learn what it means to fully love God."

Berlin compares the process of loving our neighbor to cleaning barnacles off a boat's hull: Our encounters and interactions with other people reveal where our souls are "sin-fouled." But when we dedicate ourselves to loving God by loving our neighbor, we can "unencumber our souls" and grow in holiness and freedom, with God's help. To love God and neighbor as Jesus calls us to love them "is the work of a lifetime."

Berlin challenges readers to focus throughout the day on the words, "Begin with Love." Beginning each day, each encounter, each conversation, and each action with love can keep us oriented toward the transforming love Jesus wills for us.

Materials You Will Need

- name tags (optional)
- newsprint or markerboard and markers
- timer or stopwatch
- Bibles
- paper and pens or markers

DURING THE SESSION

Opening Activity and Prayer (5-10 minutes)

Welcome participants. Introduce yourself and ask them to introduce themselves. Briefly tell participants why you are excited to be facilitating this study of Tom Berlin's book *Reckless Love*, and invite volunteers to talk about why they are interested in the study.

Set a timer for one minute. Ask participants to call out as many familiar phrases, quotes, and titles including the word "love" (or some variation) in one minute as they can. Recruit a scribe to write down responses, or write responses yourself. After calling time, invite participants to review the group list. Ask:

- Based on these responses, how would you define love?
- How much is this definition of love like or unlike your own definition?
- How much do you think this definition is like or unlike God's definition of love? Why?

Explain that this session will explore what God means when commanding us to love God and to love our neighbor.

Lead this prayer or one in your own words:

In love you created us, Holy God, and in love you intend us to live. We confess the limits of our love before you, and humbly ask you send your Spirit during this time of reading, reflection, and relationship to increase our love for you and for our neighbor—a love made real in speech and action, not in mere sentiment. May our conversations and commitments today honor you and open us to the transforming work of your Son who first loved us, Jesus Christ. Amen.

Video Presentation (15 minutes)

Play the video for Session 1. In *Reckless Love*, Tom Berlin focuses on the physical journey of Jesus and his disciples. In this 10- to 12-minute segment, Berlin embarks on a journey in a car with a friend to talk about love of God and neighbor. Take a moment to discuss points raised in the video. Groups with more time may want to extend this portion to allow for a longer conversation.

Book Discussion (15 minutes)

Read or review the summary of chapter 1. Ask participants who have read the chapter to comment briefly on what in it most interested or challenged them, and why. Then discuss the chapter in more depth, using some or all of these questions to prompt discussion:

- Tom Berlin quotes a rabbi who said Judaism's greatest contribution "was not monotheism, the belief in one god," but "ethical monotheism." What distinguishes one from the other? How do our beliefs about who God is shape the kind of people we become?
- "Israel loved the Lord because God was, in a word, *lovely.*" When, where, and how have you experienced the "loveliness" of God? How central are those experiences to your love for God? How do you love God when you *don't* experience God as lovely?
- Berlin writes, "To love God with all your being was to live God's way. This was the reason for the law and commandments." How would you describe the connection between God's law and God's love? If, as Berlin argues, God's law calls us to be better

people than we would have been on our own, what is its place in Christians' lives?

- Berlin writes "nothing reveals what keeps us from fully loving God and growing in the likeness of Christ like attempting to love our neighbor." Think about a neighbor you have found—or perhaps even still find—difficult to love. How has God used this neighbor to show you your soul's "rough spots"? Avoid naming names or pointing fingers—focus on what you have learned about the difficulties and the rewards of loving God more fully through your efforts to love this neighbor.

- Berlin identifies several spiritual practices—Bible study, prayer, worship, and others—that can act as "means of grace [to] help us grow in our love of God." Which of the means of grace he mentions have proven most important to you, and why?

- Why does Berlin say we need God in order to love our neighbors? Have you ever tried to love your neighbor relying solely on your own strength? What happened?

Bible Study (15 minutes)

Recruit volunteers to read aloud the Biblical Foundations (dividing the texts into smaller sections as desired). After each Scripture, use some or all of these questions provided to prompt discussion:

Mark 12:28-34

- In both Matthew's (22:34-40) and Luke's (10:25-28) versions of this incident, the question to Jesus about the "greatest commandment" is called a test. How is Mark's version different? How, if at all, does the difference shape your perception of the legal expert and the law?

- As Berlin notes, Jesus quotes the Shema (shuh-MAH), a foundational prayer and confession of faith in Judaism. Berlin claims Jesus' connection of the Shema (Deuteronomy 6:4) and the commandment to love our neighbors as ourselves

(Leviticus 19:18) "creates a real problem." How? How does his linking of these commandments also, as Berlin observes, create a real opportunity?

- Does the legal expert's conclusion about God valuing love more than sacrifices mean sacrifices, which God mandated in the law, are without worth? Why or why not?
- Jesus' conversation with the legal expert highlights love as the key element in living faithfully with God, despite our temptation to make things other than love central. How have you personally seen the church both forget and remember to make love most important? How have you both forgotten and remembered in your life as Jesus' follower?

Galatians 5:16-26

- The apostle Paul is confident those who "live by the Spirit" will not "gratify the desires of the flesh" (verse 16). Do you share his confidence? Why or why not?
- What does it mean, in concrete and practical terms, to "live by the Spirit"?
- Paul also contrasts being "led by the Spirit" with being "subject to the law" (verse 18). What does he mean, especially given the purpose of God's commandments to "call [us] to be a better person than [we] would have ever been on [our] own"? How, if at all, can the Spirit and the law be at odds if both are from God?
- Tom Berlin pictures the vices Paul names (verses 19-21) as "barnacles" of sin on the hull of our souls. "Over time," Berlin comments, "even one or two of the actions and attitudes that Paul observed can slow us down." Which of these "barnacles" are you aware of "sin-fouling" your soul? How did you become aware of them? What are you doing about them?
- Talk about a time when you have experienced one or more of Paul's "fruit of the Spirit" (verses 22-23). When did these

experiences occur as a result of the "virtuous cycle," as Berlin calls it, that results from loving our neighbor?

CLOSING THE SESSION

Closing Activity and Prayer (5-10 minutes)

Distribute paper to participants. Invite them to draw an image—a picture, a symbol, a decorated word or phrase—that will help them remember to begin each day, encounter, conversation, and action with love. Invite those who wish to present and talk about what they drew with the whole group. Encourage participants to display their drawings someplace they will see them every day, as a reminder of their commitment to "Begin with Love."

Lead this prayer or one in your own words:

Jesus, our loving Savior: Your call to love God and neighbor is not always, or even usually, easy to obey. We thank you for your grace, which alone allows us to grow up into the people you would have us be. By your Spirit's power, may all we have said and heard in this time that will free us from unloving ways take root in our hearts as your word to us, and when we meet again, may we have testimony to share with each other of how our love for our neighbors and our love for God has increased. Amen.

Encourage participants to exchange signs and words of peace with each other as they leave.

Extra Activity

Search online for videos and/or audio recordings of the Shema being recited in Hebrew. Look for images of Jewish *tefillin* (phylacteries) and *mezuzahs,* and find out how these objects are connected to the Shema. How does Jewish tradition and practice around the Shema reflect its importance in the Jewish faith? Do you think Christians have (or should have) an equivalent prayer and set of practices keeping our call to love God always before us?

SESSION 2
EXPAND THE CIRCLE

PLANNING THE SESSION

Session Goals

The conversations and activities in this session will equip participants to:

- Think about whether the people currently in their relational circles are like or unlike them.

- Contemplate how Jesus' call to love God and neighbor encompasses a call to love ourselves.

- Explore why and how Jesus calls us into relationship with people different from ourselves.

- Prayerfully reflect on God's deeply personal knowledge of and love for them.

18

Biblical Foundations

¹Once while Jesus was standing beside the lake of
Gennesaret, and the crowd was pressing in on him to
hear the word of God, ²he saw two boats there at the
shore of the lake; the fishermen had gone out of them
and were washing their nets. ³He got into one of the
boats, the one belonging to Simon, and asked him to
put out a little way from the shore. Then he sat down and
taught the crowds from the boat. ⁴When he had finished
speaking, he said to Simon, "Put out into the deep water
and let down your nets for a catch." ⁵Simon answered,
"Master, we have worked all night long but have caught
nothing. Yet if you say so, I will let down the nets."
⁶When they had done this, they caught so many fish that
their nets were beginning to break. ⁷So they signaled
their partners in the other boat to come and help them.
And they came and filled both boats, so that they began
to sink. ⁸But when Simon Peter saw it, he fell down at
Jesus' knees, saying, "Go away from me, Lord, for I am
a sinful man!" ⁹For he and all who were with him were
amazed at the catch of fish that they had taken; ¹⁰and so
also were James and John, sons of Zebedee, who were
partners with Simon. Then Jesus said to Simon, "Do not
be afraid; from now on you will be catching people."
¹¹When they had brought their boats to shore, they left
everything and followed him.

Luke 5:1-11

²⁷After this [Jesus] went out and saw a tax collector
named Levi, sitting at the tax booth; and he said to
him, "Follow me." ²⁸And he got up, left everything, and
followed him.

²⁹Then Levi gave a great banquet for him in his house;
and there was a large crowd of tax collectors and others

sitting at the table with them. ³⁰The Pharisees and their scribes were complaining to his disciples, saying, "Why do you eat and drink with tax collectors and sinners?" ³¹Jesus answered, "Those who are well have no need of a physician, but those who are sick; ³²I have come to call not the righteous but sinners to repentance."

Luke 5:27-32

Chapter Summary

In chapter 2, Tom Berlin tells readers that learning to truly love God and neighbor means having our relational circles expanded. "Jesus," writes Berlin, "has a way of bringing people into your life that you never expected and would have never chosen on your own."

Berlin illustrates Jesus' circle-expanding tendency with two stories from Luke 5. In the first, Jesus guides Simon Peter to a miraculous catch of fish and calls him to fish for people. Berlin focuses on the shame and guilt Simon feels in response to Jesus' invitation. Yet Jesus knows all our secrets and offers forgiveness for our guilt and healing for our shame. Jesus summons us to love ourselves—to bring ourselves, our *genuine* selves, into our relational circles. Berlin says, "In opening yourself to the love Christ has for you, loving yourself gets a whole lot easier."

In the second story from Luke 5, Jesus calls Levi the tax collector to follow him. Berlin wonders how Simon Peter reacted to being asked to follow Jesus alongside "Levi, a blood-sucking parasite who is a minion of the Empire." Berlin argues Jesus intentionally created a learning climate in which the disciples' capacity to love could expand "by putting them with people who would stretch them."

Jesus is creating that climate for us, as well. When Jesus calls you, "he doesn't tell you where you are going or who you will have to love" because "if you had that information, you would never take the journey" to become who God intends you to be.

Materials You Will Need

- name tags (optional)
- paper and pens or markers
- newsprint or markerboard and markers
- Bibles
- children's modeling compound (such as Crayola Model Magic—check local convenience stores, toy stores, or craft stores, or order online) (optional)

DURING THE SESSION

Opening Activity and Prayer (5-10 minutes)

Welcome participants, especially any who may be joining the study in this session. Invite volunteers to talk briefly about what they remember and insights they gained from the first session, and how they responded to the session in their lives.

Distribute paper and pens or pencils to participants. Guide them through the following exercise, based on Tom Berlin's discussion in chapter 2 of Dunbar's number:

- Write down the names of the five people you consider closest to you. Draw a circle around those names.
- Draw a slightly larger circle around the first. In this circle, write the names of the ten next closest people to you, your close friends.
- Draw a slightly larger third circle around the first two. In this circle, write up to twenty more names of people you know.
- Draw a slightly larger fourth, final circle. How many names can you write down of people you would recognize on sight?
- Finally, underline any name in any circle belonging to someone you would say is very different from yourself.

Ask volunteers to look at the names they have written down and think about these questions from *Reckless Love*: "Take a look at the names you have written down. What do you notice about the list? Who are these people? Where did you meet them? Why are they important to you? How much variety is there among these names in terms of where they live, where they come from, race, religious practice, identity, culture, or political ideology? Do you see more variance in your inner, middle or outer circles? In completing this exercise, many people find that their innermost circles are the most homogeneous. For some people, the whole list is similar." Invite volunteers to respond aloud to some or all of Berlin's questions.

Explain that this session will explore how and why Jesus calls us to be in relationship with people who are unlike us.

Lead this prayer or one in your own words:

God of love, you came among us in someone we would least expect: a wandering rabbi from Nazareth who brought together an unlikely assortment of fishermen, tax collectors, and sinners to form a holy community. As we, too, come together at your call, we ask your Spirit to guide our time together, shaping and stretching us into more faithful disciples who grow in our ability to love everyone you place in our lives. Amen.

Video Presentation (15 minutes)

Play the video for Session 2. In *Reckless Love*, Tom Berlin focuses on the physical journey of Jesus and his disciples. In this 10- to 12-minute segment, Berlin continues his car trip with another guest as they talk about various kinds of relationships. Take a moment to discuss points raised in the video. Groups with more time may want to extend this portion to allow for a longer conversation.

Book Discussion (15 minutes)

Read or review the summary of chapter 2. Ask participants who have read the chapter to comment briefly on what in it most interested or challenged them, and why. Then discuss the chapter in more depth, using some or all of these questions to prompt discussion:

- Berlin draws a distinction between the experiences of shame (when "people treated you as something less than a child of God") and guilt ("things we did all on our own that wounded ourselves or others"). Shame needs healing and guilt needs forgiveness, but both can cause us to withdraw from our neighbor and from God. What experiences can you share, from your own or from others' experiences, of healing and forgiveness breaking shame and guilt's power to isolate us? (You need not share your response aloud, and respect others' privacy by not naming names.)
- "The only way to learn the greatest commandment," writes Berlin of the experience Jesus created when calling his first disciples, "is to have people in our lives who we personally find so difficult to love that we have to get up every morning and pray to our Creator for a love we could not produce on our own." When have you had to pray a prayer like that? Avoid naming names or making accusations in blame. Do you believe God has answered your prayer? Why or why not?
- Can trying to love someone we find difficult to love ever conflict with God's command to love ourselves? Why or why not? If we find these goals in tension with each other, how should we respond? Who can we trust to help us discern what to do?
- How does a desire for a community or a world in which everyone is alike (and like us) conflict with God's will?

Bible Study (15 minutes)

Recruit volunteers to read aloud the Biblical Foundations (dividing the texts into smaller sections as desired). Consider recruiting different readers to read each of the "roles" in these two stories from Luke 5. After each Scripture, use some or all of the questions provided to prompt discussion:

Luke 5:1-11

- "Those with skills and experience," Berlin writes, "do not like amateurs offering suggestions." Why do you think Simon Peter obeys Jesus' command to drop his nets in deep water (verse 5)?
- When Simon sees the miraculous catch of fish, he realizes he is in the presence of holiness and that, according to Berlin, "made him think about all the aspects of his past and present life that were unholy." When and how have you felt yourself near holiness? When, if ever, have you responded as Simon did? What other responses to holiness have you personally experienced?
- What does Jesus mean when he tells Simon he will be "catching people" (verse 10)? Tom Berlin says it represents Jesus wanting not so much to do something *with* Simon's life as *in* Simon's life. Do you agree? Why or why not?
- How could Jesus' invitation and Simon as well as the other fishermen's response to it be characterized as "reckless"? When, if ever, have you responded recklessly to Jesus? What happened (or is still happening) as a result?

Luke 5:27-32

- Luke notes Levi's call takes place "after" something (verse 27). What happened in between Jesus' calling Simon and Levi? How might these events shape the way we read the story about Levi's call?
- As Berlin notes, first-century tax collectors were hated people because they were Jews who made a living by collaborating with the Roman Empire, gathering revenue for the emperor and keeping the excess for themselves. Why does Jesus say he calls people like Levi to follow him (verses 31-32)?
- Berlin suggests Jesus called Levi to expand his disciples' relational circles and, in so doing, expand their whole beings so they could love God more fully. What other Gospel stories

can you remember or find that support this interpretation of how Jesus formed the disciples' community? How do you think Christian communities today would change, if at all, if they viewed their differences as indicators of Jesus at work, trying to expand their capacity to love God and each other?

CLOSING THE SESSION

Closing Activity and Prayer (5-10 minutes)

Give each participant a small amount of children's modeling compound and ask them to sculpt a representation of themselves. When participants have finished, ask them to stretch their sculpture as far as they can without breaking it. Ask:

- How can you tell when your figure is near its breaking point?
- Did some of your figures stretch farther or shorter than you imagined?
- How does loving other people "stretch" us?
- How does trusting in God as the source of love keep us from being stretched to our breaking point when we love others?
- How does God "reshape" us if we are broken into a new creation?

Lead this prayer or one in your own words:

Creator God, create us anew, every day, as people who receive and share your love. Show us yourself through your compassionate eyes, that we may love ourselves more fully in order to more fully love our neighbors, especially those the world and we too often consider unlovable. This we pray in the name of your love made flesh, Jesus Christ. Amen.

Encourage participants to exchange signs and words of peace with each other as they leave.

Extra Activity

Lectio divina (Latin for "divine reading") invites us to read Scripture in a contemplative way, aware of the Word's power to engage our hearts and imagination and nurture our growth as the people God wants us to become. There is no single "right way" to do *lectio*, but here is one model you and your group can try, using Psalm 139:1-12, which echoes the idea in chapter 2 of *Reckless Love* that God already knows all our secrets.

- Recruit three different volunteers to read the text aloud, one after the other—clearly, at a deliberate but not overly slow pace. Those who are not reading should not follow along in their own Bibles, but should listen attentively to the Scripture being read.
- After each reading, the leader should ask the questions below. You may wish to share these questions before beginning so participants are clear what to expect. No one must be forced to participate.
- After the first reading, invite participants to speak aloud the word, phrase, or image that most attracted their attention.
- After the second reading, allow a minute or two of silence, then ask participants to describe how they "see" or imagine themselves in the psalm. How does the text connect with their lives right now? What is God doing with or to them in the psalm? Other participants may ask questions for clarification, but not to judge what is being shared.
- After the third and final reading, allow two to three minutes of silence, then ask what participants believe or sense God is calling them to do or to be after having encountered the psalm. Other participants may ask clarifying questions, make affirmations, or offer other, non-judging perspectives.
- Close the *lectio* experience with the Lord's Prayer or another prayer familiar to your group.

SESSION 3
LAVISH LOVE

PLANNING THE SESSION

Session Goals

The conversations and activities in this session will equip participants to:

- Consider imagery to convey the force of both hate and love.
- Explore Jesus' teachings in the "Sermon on the Plain" about lavish, generous love.
- Practice observing their lives for specific signs of God's love.
- Commit themselves to small but significant actions of promoting love.

Biblical Foundations

[Jesus said,] [27]"I say to you that listen, Love your enemies, do good to those who hate you, [28]bless those who curse you, pray for those who abuse you. [29]If anyone strikes you on the cheek, offer the other also; and from

27

anyone who takes away your coat do not withhold even your shirt. [30]Give to everyone who begs from you; and if anyone takes away your goods, do not ask for them again. [31]Do to others as you would have them do to you.

[32]"If you love those who love you, what credit is that to you? For even sinners love those who love them. [33]If you do good to those who do good to you, what credit is that to you? For even sinners do the same. [34]If you lend to those from whom you hope to receive, what credit is that to you? Even sinners lend to sinners, to receive as much again. [35]But love your enemies, do good, and lend, expecting nothing in return. Your reward will be great, and you will be children of the Most High; for he is kind to the ungrateful and the wicked. [36]Be merciful, just as your Father is merciful.

[37]"Do not judge, and you will not be judged; do not condemn, and you will not be condemned. Forgive, and you will be forgiven; [38]give, and it will be given to you. A good measure, pressed down, shaken together, running over, will be put into your lap; for the measure you give will be the measure you get back."

Luke 6:27-38

[1]Bless the LORD, O my soul,
    and all that is within me,
    bless his holy name.
[2]Bless the LORD, O my soul,
    and do not forget all his benefits—
[3]who forgives all your iniquity,
    who heals all your diseases,
[4]who redeems your life from the Pit,
    who crowns you with steadfast love and mercy,
[5]who satisfies you with good as long as you live
    so that your youth is renewed like the eagle's.

⁶The Lᴏʀᴅ works vindication
    and justice for all who are oppressed.
⁷He made known his ways to Moses,
    his acts to the people of Israel.
⁸The Lᴏʀᴅ is merciful and gracious,
    slow to anger and abounding in steadfast love.
⁹He will not always accuse,
    nor will he keep his anger forever.
¹⁰He does not deal with us according to our sins,
    nor repay us according to our iniquities.
¹¹For as the heavens are high above the earth,
    so great is his steadfast love toward those who
    fear him;
¹²as far as the east is from the west,
    so far he removes our transgressions from us.
¹³As a father has compassion for his children,
    so the Lᴏʀᴅ has compassion for those who fear him.
¹⁴For he knows how we were made;
    he remembers that we are dust.

Psalm 103:1-14

Chapter Summary

All God's children need to be taught how to love. Tom Berlin identifies lessons in love as the core of Jesus' teaching. He considers Jesus' "Sermon on the Plain" an "orientation lecture" about the life of love characterizing the kingdom of God. Jesus wanted, and wants, his followers "to learn to be the most loving people on the planet."

As human beings stuck in an ongoing "struggle to gain the upper hand," we still need to increase our capacity to love. Berlin discusses the October 2018 mass shooting at Tree of Life Synagogue in Pittsburgh, Pennsylvania, as an especially heinous example of hatred's persistence. Berlin points out all of us experience hatred within ourselves, usually in smaller but no less real ways. God calls us to act in love instead—as Dr. Jeff Cohen, a Tree of

Life member, did when he visited the shooter in the hospital; or as relatives did when they offered forgiveness to the man who murdered nine of their family members at a church Bible study at Emanuel AME Church in Charleston, South Carolina, in 2015. "When we lavish love," writes Berlin, "we offer it freely and generously, the same way that God loves us and offers us grace and forgiveness when we ask for it."

Choosing love over hate and forgiveness over resentment or revenge breaks sin's grip on us. But loving other people is hard. In order to answer Christ's call to constant love, we need Christ himself "not just to set the standard for us, but to work in our lives."

We can also develop spiritual practices to help us become more loving people. One practice Berlin suggests is observing our lives, as the author of Psalm 103 observed his. "When we observe and remember the deep love of God for us," Berlin explains, "our hearts overflow with thanksgiving that is expressed not only in words, but in our love of others." We treat others benevolently. Other people cease to be objects who matter only for the transactions we want to conduct with them, but as fellow subjects whose inherently sacred lives we honor with genuine encounters marked by compassion and concern.

Materials You Will Need

- name tags (optional)
- smart devices or multimedia computer with Internet access (optional)
- newsprint or markerboard and markers
- Bibles

DURING THE SESSION

Opening Activity and Prayer (5-10 minutes)

Welcome participants, especially any who may be joining the study in this session. Invite volunteers to talk briefly about what they remember and insights they have gained from the study so far, and how they responded to the study in their lives.

Mention that, in chapter 3 of *Reckless Love*, author Tom Berlin uses two dramatic images from the natural world, a mudslide and an avalanche. Invite participants who have seen these phenomena (or similar ones such as earthquakes or wildfires), in person or in video footage, to describe their thoughts and feelings about those experiences. Ask whether these images provoke mainly positive or negative responses in participants, and why.

Optional: Before the session, choose an online video of a mudslide or an avalanche to show during this activity.

Explain that Berlin uses these natural images as metaphors for destructive emotion and action: "a mudslide of hate," "an avalanche of hate and violence." Tell participants this session will examine why he does so, but will also explore images illustrating the forceful but positive power of love.

Lead this prayer or one in your own words:

Holy God, in your world, love is the hallmark of true living. In this fallen and broken world, we yearn for lives suffused with that love, but we find it so hard, so much of the time, to let your Spirit shape us into more loving people. We offer this time of reading and reflection to you as a small but significant token of our desire to grow into the loving followers of Jesus you want us to become. Through it, may you move us from desire to "doing," from aspiration to action, that we may reflect your love to all around us. Amen.

Video Presentation (15 minutes)

Play the video for Session 3. In *Reckless Love*, Tom Berlin focuses on the physical journey of Jesus and his disciples. In this 10- to 12-minute segment, Berlin chats with a guest on a car ride about what lavish love can look like. Take a moment to discuss points raised in the video. Groups with more time may want to extend this portion to allow for a longer conversation.

Book Discussion (15 minutes)

Read or review the summary of chapter 3. Ask participants who have read the chapter to comment briefly on what in it most interested or challenged them, and why. Then discuss the chapter in more depth, using some or all of these questions to prompt discussion:

- Why does Berlin say the two young sisters he observed in the airport illustrate "the human condition"? When have you witnessed people's "struggle to gain the upper hand" for yourself?
- How is hatred like a mudslide or an avalanche, according to Berlin? What do you do when you are aware of hate's small beginnings in your own heart?
- Talk about someone you know of who, like Dr. Jeff Cohen or Bethane Middleton Brown, whose sister was murdered in the Charleston church shooting, has shown mercy and forgiveness in a "remarkable" way. Why do you think stories like theirs make such an impression on people? How, if at all, does forgiveness offered in extreme circumstances differ from forgiveness offered "for much smaller offenses"?
- "We will need to cultivate practices that keep us connected to Christ," writes Berlin, in order to answer Christ's call to constant love. What practices do you follow that keep you aware of your dependency on Jesus and his love? What other practices, if any, have you seen help others stay connected to Jesus that you would be interested in trying?
- Berlin claims an unobserved life is often an ungrateful life. How much do you agree or disagree, and why? What does "observing" your life as Berlin defines it—noting the many decisions that have shaped you into the person you have become—look like in practical terms?
- When have you experienced an "I-Thou" encounter in which you have lived into "Christ's call to lavish, constant love"?

Bible Study (15 minutes)

Recruit volunteers to read aloud the Biblical Foundations (dividing the texts into smaller sections as desired). After each Scripture, use some or all of the questions provided to prompt discussion:

Luke 6:27-38

- As Tom Berlin notes, the "Sermon on the Plain" (Luke 6:20-49) "follows the account of Jesus' call to his disciples." What significance, if any, do you find in the fact that Jesus addresses this sermon not to the multitudes who want healing from him (verses 18-19) but specifically to "his disciples" (verse 20)?
- Berlin characterizes Jesus' sermon as an "orientation lecture" for life in God's kingdom. How do the sermon's initial teachings in verses 20-26 orient Jesus' disciples to values and priorities that distinguish God's realm from earthly realms?
- "The most common topic in the [Sermon on the Plain] is love," writes Berlin. What's the connection between this topic when Jesus introduces it (starting at verse 27) and what he has been talking about before?
- How do the practical examples of love Jesus discusses exemplify the lavish nature of the godly love he wants his followers to practice?
- When, if ever, have you been the recipient of this kind of generous love that expects "nothing in return" (verse 35)?
- Do you think the expectation of receiving a great reward (verse 35) from God for showing love diminishes that love's lavish nature? Why or why not?
- Which of Jesus' practical examples of love do you find most challenging to live out? Why?

Psalm 103:1-14

- What specific "benefits" from God does the psalmist note when observing his or her life? How many, if any, of these same benefits are you able to identify when you observe your own life, or the lives of those around you?

- The psalmist calls for wholehearted praise of God (verse 1). What does it look, sound, and feel like when everything within us blesses God's name? How is such praise a way to love God?
- How does Psalm 103 illustrate the importance of knowing God's past with God's people when we want to remember God's benefits? How can this knowledge sustain us if we have trouble observing God's benefits in our own experience?
- Berlin states one of Psalm 103's "most important observations" about God is God's *hesed* (verse 8), or "steadfast [constant] love." How does the psalmist define and describe God's *hesed*? What motivates God's loyal love? What is or ought to be the relationship between God's *hesed* and our own?
- What human relationship does the psalmist use as an analogy for God's lavish love? What other human relationships would you suggest as images of God's love, and why?

CLOSING THE SESSION

Closing Activity and Prayer (5-10 minutes)

According to Tom Berlin, both love and hate can start small, "but if fed and nurtured...will grow considerably." Ask participants to identify one small but significant thing they will do before the next session to feed and nurture their love for other people. Suggest your group's actions can, combined, help create a forceful, constructive expression of love. Ask what images from nature might communicate that reality, in contrast to the destructive images of hate's power (the mudslide, the avalanche).

Lead this prayer or one in your own words:

Compassionate God, we can love only because you have first loved us. When we find your call to love each other challenging, and when we are tempted to yield to stirrings of anger and hate in our hearts, may your Spirit again bring us back to the cross of Christ, where we see how greatly we have been forgiven and loved, and so how greatly we must forgive and love. Amen.

Encourage participants to exchange signs and words of peace with each other as they leave.

Extra Activity

Ignatius of Loyola (1491-1556), the Spanish Roman Catholic priest who founded the Jesuit order, developed a spiritual discipline he called "the examen" as a way of reviewing each day for signs of God's presence and activity in the believer's life. The examen can be one way of "observing" our lives, as Berlin urges us to do.

The examen is a three-part period of prayer and meditation at the close of day. Here is an adaptation of the examen, using some language and ideas from Psalm 103 and chapter 3 of *Reckless Love*.

- Pray for God to make you aware of the moment from the day for which you were most grateful. How, specifically, did you receive God's "benefits" in this moment? Give wholehearted thanks to God for this moment and the blessings it contained.
- Pray for God to make you aware of the moment from the day for which you were least grateful. How was this moment like being in "the Pit" of which the psalmist sang? As you recall the moment, ask God to lift you out of it now and to lavish divine compassion on you, so you may treat yourself and any others involved in that moment compassionately and without anger or hatred.
- Close by thanking God for whatever you have seen and felt as you observed your life in this examen. Write down some brief thoughts about how God has used this time to reveal the unique pattern of your life to you. If possible, discuss your thoughts with another Christian. Prayerfully consider how you can use your insights to lavish love on others tomorrow.

SESSION 4
OPENHEARTED LOVE

PLANNING THE SESSION

Session Goals

The conversations and activities in this session will equip participants to:

- Discuss "agitation" as an important way God teaches us how to love and as our response to God's love.
- Explain how Jesus challenged biased and prejudiced social norms in his interactions with Samaritans in John 4.
- Articulate what it means to be an "ambassador" for Christ, as Paul teaches in 2 Corinthians 5.
- Examine their own lives for prejudices and biases, and commit to challenging them in practical ways.

Biblical Foundations

⁴[Jesus] had to go through Samaria. ⁵So he came to a Samaritan city called Sychar, near the plot of ground that

Jacob had given to his son Joseph. ⁶Jacob's well was there, and Jesus, tired out by his journey, was sitting by the well. It was about noon.

⁷A Samaritan woman came to draw water, and Jesus said to her, "Give me a drink." ⁸(His disciples had gone to the city to buy food.) ⁹The Samaritan woman said to him, "How is it that you, a Jew, ask a drink of me, a woman of Samaria?" (Jews do not share things in common with Samaritans.) ¹⁰Jesus answered her, "If you knew the gift of God, and who it is that is saying to you, 'Give me a drink,' you would have asked him, and he would have given you living water." ¹¹The woman said to him, "Sir, you have no bucket, and the well is deep. Where do you get that living water? ¹²Are you greater than our ancestor Jacob, who gave us the well, and with his sons and his flocks drank from it?" ¹³Jesus said to her, "Everyone who drinks of this water will be thirsty again, ¹⁴but those who drink of the water that I will give them will never be thirsty. The water that I will give will become in them a spring of water gushing up to eternal life." ¹⁵The woman said to him, "Sir, give me this water, so that I may never be thirsty or have to keep coming here to draw water."

¹⁶Jesus said to her, "Go, call your husband, and come back." ¹⁷The woman answered him, "I have no husband." Jesus said to her, "You are right in saying, 'I have no husband'; ¹⁸for you have had five husbands, and the one you have now is not your husband. What you have said is true!" ¹⁹The woman said to him, "Sir, I see that you are a prophet. ²⁰Our ancestors worshiped on this mountain, but you say that the place where people must worship is in Jerusalem." ²¹Jesus said to her, "Woman, believe me, the hour is coming when you will worship the Father neither on this mountain nor in

Jerusalem. [22]You worship what you do not know; we worship what we know, for salvation is from the Jews. [23]But the hour is coming, and is now here, when the true worshipers will worship the Father in spirit and truth, for the Father seeks such as these to worship him. [24]God is spirit, and those who worship him must worship in spirit and truth." [25]The woman said to him, "I know that Messiah is coming" (who is called Christ). "When he comes, he will proclaim all things to us." [26]Jesus said to her, "I am he, the one who is speaking to you."

[27]Just then his disciples came. They were astonished that he was speaking with a woman, but no one said, "What do you want?" or, "Why are you speaking with her?" [28]Then the woman left her water jar and went back to the city. She said to the people, [29]"Come and see a man who told me everything I have ever done! He cannot be the Messiah, can he?" [30]They left the city and were on their way to him....

[40]So when the Samaritans came to him, they asked him to stay with them; and he stayed there two days.

John 4:4-30, 40

[18]All this is from God, who reconciled us to himself through Christ, and has given us the ministry of reconciliation; [19]that is, in Christ God was reconciling the world to himself, not counting their trespasses against them, and entrusting the message of reconciliation to us. [20]So we are ambassadors for Christ, since God is making his appeal through us; we entreat you on behalf of Christ, be reconciled to God. [21]For our sake he made him to be sin who knew no sin, so that in him we might become the righteousness of God.

2 Corinthians 5:18-21

Chapter Summary

A trip to tour Cedar Hill, the home of famous Civil War–era abolitionist Frederick Douglass, prompted Tom Berlin to consider two meanings of the word *agitate*, which Douglass used to summarize his life's work. It can mean to confront and challenge; it can also mean to cleanse. "To be agitated," Berlin writes, "is to have our lives cleansed of what inhibits God's love from radiating from our lives."

Berlin argues Jesus led his disciples on a journey meant to agitate them when he traveled through Samaria. Jesus knew his followers would encounter "people and situations that confronted their most deeply held beliefs and biases about other people," beliefs and biases holding them back from the "openhearted living" that characterizes life in God's kingdom.

Jesus' conversation with the woman at the well forced his disciples to confront their views about gender, Berlin states, because "while the Hebrew Bible offered stories of important women,...there was also a great deal of negative teaching about women in Jewish culture at that time." And Jesus' decision to accept the Samaritans' invitation to stay forced his disciples to confront their views about race because of the prejudices they likely held about Samaritans: "Jewish people of Jesus' time judged the people of Samaria to be idolaters, ceremonially unclean, and socially unsavory." But Jesus, unhindered by cultural bias or stereotypes, knew "persistent agitation can open even the most tightly closed of hearts."

Berlin challenges readers to identify their own "village in Samaria"— a place they would not want Jesus to call them to go because of their own biases and bigotry. Christians are, as Paul writes to the Corinthians, called to be Christ's ambassadors, representing Jesus everywhere and with everyone as we pursue the reconciliation with our neighbors that our reconciliation with God demands.

Berlin identifies four spiritual practices to help us make the changes we need to make to love our neighbors, and so love God, more fully:

- Be intentional about examining prejudice, hatred, and injustice.
- Be vulnerable and acknowledge prejudice and its past and present effects.
- Be confessional about how we have been closing and continue to close our hearts to others.
- Be active in taking risks to achieve reconciliation.

Materials You Will Need

- name tags (optional)
- newsprint or markerboard and markers
- Bibles
- scrap paper

DURING THE SESSION

Opening Activity and Prayer (5-10 minutes)

Welcome participants, especially any who may be joining the study in this session. Invite volunteers to talk briefly about what they remember and insights they have gained from the study so far, and how they responded to the study in their lives.

Ask participants: "What is a historic site or museum you've visited that made an emotional impact on you, and why?" (If you need to broaden the question, ask about places important in participants' personal or family pasts.) After participants respond, explain that Tom Berlin begins chapter 4 by talking about the emotional impact visiting Frederick Douglass's home had on him. Tell participants this session is about turning emotional impact into practical action that helps us grow in our love for our neighbors and for God.

Lead this prayer or one in your own words:

God of all, from whom every family on earth receives its name: How quick we are to say we love you, but how slow we often are to love our neighbors! We dare ask you to stir up your Holy Spirit within and among us in this time of study, that we may more fully open our hearts to the people—all people—around us, and so more fully open our hearts to you. This we pray in the name of the One close to your heart, who makes you known, Jesus Christ our Savior. Amen.

Video Presentation (15 minutes)

Play the video for Session 4. In *Reckless Love*, Tom Berlin focuses on the physical journey of Jesus and his disciples. In this 10- to 12-minute segment, Berlin's car journey continues as he talks to a guest about the value of agitation and openhearted love. Take a moment to discuss points raised in the video. Groups with more time may want to extend this portion to allow for a longer conversation.

Book Discussion (15 minutes)

Read or review the summary of chapter 4. Ask participants who have read the chapter to comment briefly on what in it most interested or challenged them, and why. Then discuss the chapter in more depth, using some or all of these questions to prompt discussion:

- According to Berlin, overcoming bias and prejudice about gender and race is "foundational" in fulfilling the command to love God and neighbor. Do you agree? Why or why not?
- Berlin relates an incident from his mission trip to Mexico that challenged a stereotype about Mexicans. Talk about a time when your ideas about a group of people were challenged. How did you respond? How does that incident influence your attitudes and actions today?
- "Throughout my lifetime," writes Berlin, "America has been a place of tension and conflict over issues of race and racial justice." How have you experienced America's racial tension and conflict: Closely? At a distance? As a victim of prejudice? As a beneficiary of historic patterns of racial advantage? Would you say racial conflict has gotten better or worse in America in your lifetime? Why?

- Berlin spends much of chapter 4 discussing his attempts to understand racism in his home state of Virginia and his efforts to come to terms with prejudice in his family's and his own past. How has prejudice been a part of your family's story? How has it been a part of your personal past? What steps, if any, have you taken to address prejudice's presence in your past and its continuing effects?
- Berlin calls Frederick Douglass an "agitator" because Douglass worked "to cleanse the soul of the nation from the stains of slavery and inequality to bring the beauty of justice to the fabric of our society." What other Americans, present or past, would you call "agitators" in the same sense? When, if ever, have you been an "agitator" like this?

Bible Study (15 minutes)

Recruit volunteers to read aloud the Biblical Foundations (dividing the texts into smaller sections as desired). When reading the passage from John 4, consider recruiting volunteers to read the "roles" of Jesus and the woman at the well. After each Scripture, use some or all of the questions provided to prompt discussion:

John 4:4-30, 40
- "When your heart is closed to a whole race of people," writes Berlin, "you will go out of your way to avoid them, even if it means the long way home to Galilee." Who are "Samaritans" in your life you have gone (or still go) out of your way to avoid? Have you ever surprised others or yourself by engaging with them, as Jesus engaged with the woman at the well?
- What have you heard taught or preached about the woman at the well that isn't supported by the Bible's text? How does drawing this distinction help highlight bias and prejudice about gender?
- How does Jesus show this woman the respect Berlin says first-century Jewish society didn't always give women? Do you

think women's status in our society is "generally inferior to that of men," as in Jesus' day? Why or why not?

- "Jesus is not great at small talk," writes Berlin. What are the "real and important" issues he discusses with the woman? How can talking about "real and important" things with others be a way of loving them?
- Why did Jesus' disciples say nothing to him about his conversation with the woman, even though it "astonished" them (verse 27)? Do you interpret their silence as a neutral, positive, or negative response? Why?
- The Samaritans' invitation to Jesus likely "agitated" the prejudices they held about Jews (verse 40). In your own experience, when have you seen one loving encounter help others happen?

2 Corinthians 5:18-21

- What character traits and qualifications are important for being a good ambassador? How are they like and/or unlike what is needed to be a good ambassador for Christ?
- What does reconciliation with God mean (verse 20)? What does it look like in practical, everyday ways? What's the connection between being reconciled to God and to our neighbor?
- Berlin considers Christ's appeal for reconciliation in the context of our society's need for racial reconciliation. How does racial reconciliation demonstrate "the righteousness of God" (verse 21)?
- Berlin describes Robert Carter III's emancipation of slaves as an example of racial reconciliation, "something monumental as a response to the lordship of Christ in his life." Who would you point to, from history or from your own experience, as someone who seriously heeded God's call to reconciliation and made personal, costly changes, on a "monumental" scale or not, to obey it?
- In what other areas of society, in addition to race and gender, is reconciliation needed? What are you doing to be Christ's ambassador in those areas?

CLOSING THE SESSION

Closing Activity and Prayer (5-10 minutes)

Distribute scrap paper. Remind participants of the four spiritual practices Berlin discusses as chapter 4 ends: intentionality, vulnerability, confession, and acts of reconciliation. Berlin pictures them as the fins of a washing machine's agitator. Encourage participants to think about one of these four "fins" and to write on their piece of paper one practical way they will engage in that spiritual practice before the next session. Ask any willing volunteers to talk about the action they are choosing to take; be ready to talk about your own response.

Lead this prayer or one in your own words:

For too long, loving God, we have been content to accept the status quo. For too long we have accepted without question the stereotypes and prejudices others around us hold. For too long we have been afraid to examine and repent of our own bias and tolerance of injustice. Send us out from this session agitated enough by your Spirit to take risks for righteousness and to show the world how following Jesus the Savior can draw neighbors closer to each other and to you. Amen.

Encourage participants to exchange signs and words of peace with each other as they leave.

Extra Activity

Berlin lists these women whom the Hebrew Bible presents positively: Ruth, Esther, Deborah, Jael, and the woman in Proverbs 31. Explain these women's significance in a few sentences. How could each of these biblical women be considered an "agitator," as Berlin uses the term in chapter 4? Use a Bible concordance, commentary, or other reference for information as necessary.

SESSION 5
VALUE THE VULNERABLE

PLANNING THE SESSION

Session Goals

The conversations and activities in this session will equip participants to:

- Identify groups of vulnerable "outsiders" in Jesus' day and in our own to whom Jesus calls his followers to extend God's love.
- Interpret Jesus' healing of a demon-possessed man in Mark as a model for engaging and loving vulnerable people.
- Commit to specific ways of loving vulnerable people in their lives and communities.

Biblical Foundation

¹They came to the other side of the sea, to the country
of the Gerasenes. ²And when he had stepped out of
the boat, immediately a man out of the tombs with an
unclean spirit met him. ³He lived among the tombs;
and no one could restrain him any more, even with a
chain; ⁴for he had often been restrained with shackles
and chains, but the chains he wrenched apart, and
the shackles he broke in pieces; and no one had the
strength to subdue him. ⁵Night and day among the
tombs and on the mountains he was always howling and
bruising himself with stones. ⁶When he saw Jesus from a
distance, he ran and bowed down before him; ⁷and he
shouted at the top of his voice, "What have you to do
with me, Jesus, Son of the Most High God? I adjure you
by God, do not torment me." ⁸For he had said to him,
"Come out of the man, you unclean spirit!" ⁹Then Jesus
asked him, "What is your name?" He replied, "My name
is Legion; for we are many." ¹⁰He begged him earnestly
not to send them out of the country. ¹¹Now there on
the hillside a great herd of swine was feeding; ¹²and the
unclean spirits begged him, "Send us into the swine; let
us enter them." ¹³So he gave them permission. And the
unclean spirits came out and entered the swine; and the
herd, numbering about two thousand, rushed down the
steep bank into the sea, and were drowned in the sea.

¹⁴The swineherds ran off and told it in the city and in the
country. Then people came to see what it was that had
happened. ¹⁵They came to Jesus and saw the demoniac
sitting there, clothed and in his right mind, the very man
who had had the legion; and they were afraid. ¹⁶Those
who had seen what had happened to the demoniac and
to the swine reported it. ¹⁷Then they began to beg Jesus

to leave their neighborhood. [18]As he was getting into the boat, the man who had been possessed by demons begged him that he might be with him. [19]But Jesus refused, and said to him, "Go home to your friends, and tell them how much the Lord has done for you, and what mercy he has shown you." [20]And he went away and began to proclaim in the Decapolis how much Jesus had done for him; and everyone was amazed.

Mark 5:1-20

Chapter Summary

Tom Berlin describes a trap "religious people" often fall into: deciding "who's in" and "who's out" when it comes to God's love. Sadly, "religious people" often decide vulnerable people are "out." "If we get really good at saying who is out," Berlin wryly observes, "we can whittle down considerably the number of people we believe God calls us to love."

In Jesus' day, some Pharisees and other Jewish religious leaders displayed this tendency. But Jesus' love "was free of categories and distinctions of who was more or less deserving" of it. Whether they were branded by others as "sinners," treated as social outcasts because of circumstances they could not control (like contagious disease or abnormal behavior attributed to demonic possession), regarded as outside God's people because of being Gentiles (non-Jews), or assumed to be cursed by God because they were poor, these vulnerable people found themselves valued by Jesus, who made them a priority in his ministry. He "saw their intrinsic value, the image of God that was imprinted upon their lives."

Berlin stresses Jesus wanted and wants his followers to be door openers, not gatekeepers. He calls us to actively invite and welcome vulnerable people into life-changing experiences of God's love. As a case in point, Berlin discusses Jesus' healing of the Gerasene man possessed by a demon. Unlike other people, Jesus does not ignore the suffering man. He frees the man from what is troubling him. And he gives the man a mission after healing him, to go and tell others about what God has done for him. "The critical power that Jesus can offer us," Berlin observes, "is the ability to love others because we see the value of not only who they are, but who, with God's help, they can be."

What practical steps can Christians take to love vulnerable people? Berlin suggests four:

- **Be Curious**: Instead of judging and rejecting others, show interest in them as they are and ask questions that will help you discover their stories: "Knowing people's stories ignites the caring God desires for us to extend."
- **Engage**: Instead of ignoring vulnerable people, actively reach out to them, even if it involves your discomfort and risk.
- **Have Expectations**: When helping vulnerable people, remember "you cannot do for others what they will not do for themselves." With some exceptions, people must be "active participant[s] in their own rescue."
- **Be Kind**: When we make Christ's love the rule in our lives, acts of kindness become more and more natural to us. Even small kind acts can have significant positive consequences.

Berlin also reminds readers in this chapter that we are *all* vulnerable people in some way. Our vulnerabilities—"the stuff we hope to disguise, ignore, and never disclose"—are what allow us to bless others, with God's help.

Materials You Will Need

- name tags (optional)
- newsprint or marker board and markers
- Bibles
- scrap paper

DURING THE SESSION

Opening Activity and Prayer (5-10 minutes)

Welcome participants, especially any who may be joining the study in this session. Invite volunteers to talk briefly about what they remember and insights they have gained from the study so far, and how they responded to the study in their lives.

Invite participants to remember a time in their lives when they were aware of being an "outsider." Ask questions to prompt them to share specific details. What were the circumstances? How was their "outsider" status communicated to them, both overtly and implicitly? How did they respond?

Now ask them to remember a time when they were aware of being an "insider." Again, elicit specific responses. How was their "insider" status communicated not only to them, but also to any "outsiders"? How comfortable or uncomfortable with being an "insider" in the situation were they, and why? (As leader, be prepared to answer both of these prompts from your own experience to model and encourage discussion.)

Tell participants Tom Berlin challenges us to draw no distinctions between "insiders" and "outsiders" where God's love is concerned. In chapter 5 of *Reckless Love*, he prompts readers to examine their own assumptions about the character of God's love and offers practical guidance for extending God's love to people who are vulnerable.

Lead this prayer or one in your own words:

Generous God, you open your arms in love wider than we could ever open ours, or than we even often dare. May we sense the gracious presence of your Spirit in this time together, that we may discover ways to make the circles of those with whom we share your love ever larger, especially the vulnerable people in our world and in our lives who need most to feel the transforming touch of your Son, our Savior, Jesus Christ. Amen.

Video Presentation (15 minutes)

Play the video for Session 5. In *Reckless Love*, Tom Berlin focuses on the physical journey of Jesus and his disciples. In this 10- to 12-minute segment, Berlin and a guest take a car trip to discuss insiders and outsiders. Take a moment to discuss points raised in the video. Groups with more time may want to extend this portion to allow for a longer conversation.

Book Discussion (15 minutes)

Read or review the summary of chapter 5. Ask participants who have read the chapter to comment briefly on what in it most interested or challenged them, and why. Then discuss the chapter in more depth, using some or all of these questions to prompt discussion:

- The word *Pharisee* has become unfair shorthand for overscrupulous religious rule-keeping and intolerance because of some Pharisees and other Jewish religious leaders who opposed Jesus during his earthly ministry. Pharisees were committed to studying God's gift of the Law and helping *all* Jews, not just priests, observe it in their daily lives. But as Tom Berlin writes, "Those who are most committed, if not careful, can become self-righteous and begin to think that they should control the doors that determine who's in and who's out." How, if ever, have you seen this dynamic at work in your experience of religious people? Have you ever been tempted to think of yourself as a religious gatekeeper in this way? What happened?
- Review the four groups of religious "outsiders" whom Jesus regarded as "insiders" in God's love (consult chapter 5 or the Chapter Summary above). Spend some time looking through one or more Gospels for stories in which Jesus reaches out to and cares for people in each of these groups. Which of these groups do you think religious people still tend to regard as "outsiders,"

and why? What modern groups would you add to the list of "outsiders" whom Jesus would consider "insiders"?

- Berlin challenges readers to consider how many people from "outsider" groups are in their own relational circles. How would you answer his question? How likely are you to "rush to get involved" with vulnerable people?
- Berlin writes he would like to "love other people enough to go to extraordinary measures to open the door" to vulnerable people. Do you think Jesus always calls us to extraordinary degrees of involvement? Why or why not? How do we discern faithful and appropriate levels of extending love to others—and how do we discern when what *we* think is "extraordinary" is actually far less than what Jesus is calling us to do?

Bible Study (15 minutes)

Recruit volunteers to read aloud the Biblical Foundation (dividing the text into smaller sections as desired). After the reading, use some or all of the questions provided to prompt discussion:

Mark 5:1-20

- The "country of the Gerasenes" (verse 1) was Gentile territory (as the presence of people raising pigs indicates, since pigs are not kosher under Jewish dietary law). Why is it important to know this fact when reading this story?
- Why do you suppose Mark describes the demon-possessed man in such detail (verses 2-5)? How do the man's strength and the place where he lives affect our understanding of his vulnerable status in his society, as well as the practical implications of what Jesus does for him?
- Jesus' ability to command the demon possessing the man to name itself signifies Jesus' power over it (verse 9). Berlin suggests we, too, must "make an effort to learn [the] names" of the "demons" in people's lives and in our communities. What are the

names of the "demons" you see—not necessarily supernatural beings, but strong and powerful forces threatening people and the community's health and wholeness? How can "naming the demons" help us "evict them"?

- Instead of responding with joy to Jesus' healing of the man, other Gerasenes beg Jesus to go away (verse 17). Why can acts of compassion and healing for vulnerable people feel disruptive and threatening to people who aren't vulnerable? When have you seen such acts make others angry in your own experience? Have your loving actions toward someone ever made other people angry? How did you respond?

- Tom Berlin says Jesus turns down the man's request to go with him so the man can share a new story about divine power and love. What from your own story do you tell others, especially vulnerable people, about God's power and love? Are you aware of how hearing about how God has dealt with "the history and damage of your past" has brought hope to someone else—or have you ever found hope in hearing such a story from someone else?

CLOSING THE SESSION

Closing Activity and Prayer (5–10 minutes)

Distribute scrap paper to participants. Encourage them to think about a specific vulnerable person in their life or their community whom they are helping or would like to help. Review the four practical ways Tom Berlin suggests Christians take to love vulnerable people: Be Curious, Engage, Have Expectations, and Be Kind. Give participants 5-7 minutes to write down a sentence or two about how each of these practical suggestions translates into a specific way they can love the vulnerable person. Assure participants they won't have to show their responses to anyone else unless they wish to. Tell participants when you lead this session's closing prayer, you will leave periods of silence during which they can use the sentences they have written as a silent or spoken petition.

Lead this prayer or one in your own words:

(*Note*: In this session's closing prayer, leave a period of silence after each bullet point for participants to use the sentences they wrote in the Closing Activity as the basis for a silent or spoken petition.)

Almighty God, in Jesus you made yourself vulnerable for our sake, and to bring us back into relationship with you. We pray for your Holy Spirit's guidance and support as we strive to love others with your all-embracing love, especially the vulnerable people we are often too quick to count as outsiders.

- *May we express curiosity about their stories and their lives...*

- *May we engage unfamiliar people and situations...*

- *May we have expectations for the people we help to take part in their healing...*

- *May we act with kindness...*

We praise you for including us in the circle of your love, O God, and commit ourselves to loving the vulnerable ones to whom you have joined us in Jesus Christ. Amen.

Encourage participants to exchange signs and words of peace with each other as they leave.

Extra Activity

Like the Gerasenes, writes Berlin, we often "prefer to turn a blind eye to the demons...in our larger community, rather than make an effort to learn their names and evict them." Challenge participants to write a letter to the editor of a local newspaper about a metaphorical "demon" in the community—a problem threatening the well-being of the community's vulnerable members. Encourage them:

- to support the claims they make about the problem and its importance with factual information and/or personal experience
- to advocate for a specific action the community should take together to address the problem (in other words, more than "someone should do something about…")
- to explain their concern about the problem with reference to their faith.

SESSION 6
EMULATE CHRIST

PLANNING THE SESSION

Session Goals

The conversations and activities in this session will equip participants to:

- Reflect on the example of love Jesus set for his disciples when he
  washed their feet.
- Interpret Jesus' parable of the Last Judgment as guidance for
  loving God and neighbor.
- Articulate their understandings of Jesus' message about losing life
  in order to find it.
- Recognize opportunities to demonstrate love for God and
  neighbor in practical ways.

Biblical Foundations

[1]Before the festival of the Passover, Jesus knew that his
hour had come to depart from this world and go to the

Father. Having loved his own who were in the world, he loved them to the end. ²The devil had already put it into the heart of Judas son of Simon Iscariot to betray him. And during supper ³Jesus, knowing that the Father had given all things into his hands, and that he had come from God and was going to God, ⁴got up from the table, took off his outer robe, and tied a towel around himself. ⁵Then he poured water into a basin and began to wash the disciples' feet and to wipe them with the towel that was tied around him. ⁶He came to Simon Peter, who said to him, "Lord, are you going to wash my feet?" ⁷Jesus answered, "You do not know now what I am doing, but later you will understand." ⁸Peter said to him, "You will never wash my feet." Jesus answered, "Unless I wash you, you have no share with me." ⁹Simon Peter said to him, "Lord, not my feet only but also my hands and my head!" ¹⁰Jesus said to him, "One who has bathed does not need to wash, except for the feet, but is entirely clean. And you are clean, though not all of you." ¹¹For he knew who was to betray him; for this reason he said, "Not all of you are clean."

¹²After he had washed their feet, had put on his robe, and had returned to the table, he said to them, "Do you know what I have done to you? ¹³You call me Teacher and Lord—and you are right, for that is what I am. ¹⁴So if I, your Lord and Teacher, have washed your feet, you also ought to wash one another's feet. ¹⁵For I have set you an example, that you also should do as I have done to you. ¹⁶Very truly, I tell you, servants are not greater than their master, nor are messengers greater than the one who sent them. ¹⁷If you know these things, you are blessed if you do them."

³⁴"I give you a new commandment, that you love one another. Just as I have loved you, you also should love

one another. [35]By this everyone will know that you are my disciples, if you have love for one another."

John 13:1-17, 34-35

[34]"Then the king will say to those at his right hand, 'Come, you that are blessed by my Father, inherit the kingdom prepared for you from the foundation of the world; [35]for I was hungry and you gave me food, I was thirsty and you gave me something to drink, I was a stranger and you welcomed me, [36]I was naked and you gave me clothing, I was sick and you took care of me, I was in prison and you visited me.' [37]Then the righteous will answer him, 'Lord, when was it that we saw you hungry and gave you food, or thirsty and gave you something to drink? [38]And when was it that we saw you a stranger and welcomed you, or naked and gave you clothing? [39]And when was it that we saw you sick or in prison and visited you?' [40]And the king will answer them, 'Truly I tell you, just as you did it to one of the least of these who are members of my family, you did it to me.'"

Matthew 25:34-40

[23]Then [Jesus] said to them all, "If any want to become my followers, let them deny themselves and take up their cross daily and follow me. [24]For those who want to save their life will lose it, and those who lose their life for my sake will save it. [25]What does it profit them if they gain the whole world, but lose or forfeit themselves?"

Luke 9:23-25

Chapter Summary

Tom Berlin invites readers to consider Jesus' hands. All Jesus did with his hands during his earthly ministry—healing, feeding, serving; ultimately, suffering as they were nailed to his cross—revealed the love in his heart.

57

To obey the Great Commandment, we must have the same "correlation" between our hands and heart.

As he told his disciples when he washed their feet, Jesus set a high standard of love for them, and us, to meet. He calls his followers not simply to "singular acts of kindness," but to a life and witness defined by love. Berlin explores Christians' calling with the metaphor of boat owners being told, "You are responsible for your own wake." We must make a "consistent and conscious effort" to not only avoid harming others but also actively serve others in love. We must emulate Jesus.

We must emulate not only Jesus' love-filled life but also his love-filled death. Jesus' own cross was a unique and "solitary experience," but he calls on all his followers to take up crosses and "die," for "without death, there can be no new life." We emulate Jesus' death when we intentionally sacrifice "those parts of our nature that are contrary to love." But this sacrificial death leads to new life, as surely as Jesus' own death led to his resurrection. This death leads to us becoming *more* ourselves, not less: "We gain the capacity to take on the true beauty of the identity God designed for us."

Berlin argues we must understand what Jesus gained for us in his death as much more than "an entry ticket into heaven." Jesus gained for us the possibility of transformation. That outcome is why deciding to accept Jesus' love is "the singular most important decision for those who want to love God, neighbor, and self consistently." Entering into that relationship with Christ enables us to BE LOVE:

Begin with Love
Expand the Circle

Lavish Love
Openhearted Love
Value the Vulnerable
Emulate Christ

The journey toward the goal to "be love" begins with the realization that we are already "beloved" by God.

Materials You Will Need

- name tags (optional)
- newsprint or marker board and markers
- timer (stopwatch)
- Bibles

DURING THE SESSION

Welcome and Opening Activity

Welcome participants to this final session in your study together of *Reckless Love*. Invite them to raise any questions or comments related to previous sessions that they want to be sure to address. If you don't think the group can or should take the time to discuss all these conversational "leftovers" at this point, write them down and be sure to come back to them, either at the end of the session or one-on-one after the study is over.

Set a timer for two minutes. Invite participants to look—*really* look—at their hands for that time. When two minutes are over, invite them to share observations about their hands. Encourage detailed and specific responses. Ask: "What, if anything, do you think your hands show yourself or others about your heart?"

Read aloud this quote from *Reckless Love*: "Jesus shows us the hands and heart of love.... [W]e cannot have Jesus' hands without Jesus' heart, and we probably won't cultivate Jesus' heart until our hands are accustomed to working in the ways of Christ." Tell participants this session will explore connections between how our hands, as symbols of all we do in our lives, express the love for God and neighbor in our hearts.

Opening Prayer

Lead this prayer or one in your own words:

Creator God, in love your hands fashioned us, and in love your Son stretched out his hands on the cross to save us and refashion us as your people. By your

Spirit, may we raise our hands and hearts to you in this time we have together, that we may more fully answer your love with the work of our hands. Amen.

Video Presentation (15 minutes)

Play the video for Session 6. In *Reckless Love*, Tom Berlin focuses on the physical journey of Jesus and his disciples. In this 10- to 12-minute segment, Berlin takes another car trip with a guest to discuss what it means to emulate the example of Christ. Take a moment to discuss points raised in the video. Groups with more time may want to extend this portion to allow for a longer conversation.

Book Discussion (15 minutes)

Read or review the summary of chapter 6. Ask participants who have read the chapter to comment briefly on what in it most interested or challenged them, and why. Then discuss the chapter in more depth, using some or all of these questions to prompt discussion:

- What's the hardest task you've ever accomplished or the highest standard you feel you've ever met? What lessons from these experiences do you think you could apply to consistently loving God and neighbor, which Berlin calls "one of the most difficult" things God asks us to do?
- Berlin reflects on how the sign he saw in a boat marina, "You are responsible for your own wake," applies to our lives. How easy or difficult do you find it to take responsibility for your "wake"? Why? Who would say you leave a "wake of love" behind you, and who would not?
- What practices have you adopted and what habits have you developed that help you more closely emulate Jesus on a daily basis?
- Opportunities to obey Christ's rule of love present themselves constantly, Berlin notes. What were some of the opportunities you were presented with over the past week? Which ones did you take? Which ones did you not? Why?

- "Jesus did not die to give us an entry ticket into heaven," writes Berlin. "He died so that we could transform." Do you agree or disagree with Berlin's statement, and why?

Bible Study (15 minutes)

Recruit volunteers to read aloud the Biblical Foundations (dividing the text into smaller sections as desired). After the readings, use some or all of the questions provided to prompt discussion:

John 13:1-17, 34-35

- What does it mean to say God has "given all things into [Jesus'] hands" (verse 3)? How do Jesus' actions at the meal with his disciples show what he thinks it means? How do you react to the idea that you, as part of "all things," have been given into Jesus' hands?
- Why does John describe Jesus' actions at this meal so deliberately and in such detail (verses 4-5)? What makes Jesus' actions so notable and unusual?
- Why does Peter object to what Jesus is doing? Have you ever objected to someone who is trying to serve you in love? Why? Has anyone ever objected to your attempts to serve her or him in love? How did you respond? What happened?
- Jesus tells his disciples he is setting an example of loving service for them to follow. What are some specific ways in which you strive to follow Jesus' example "day after day...in both good seasons and bad"?
- Tom Berlin notes the "power of [the] servant-oriented act" of washing feet does not always translate easily to our modern culture, where shoes cover people's feet and keep them clean. What physical actions do you think might communicate Jesus' message of loving service more readily today?

- As Berlin explains, Jesus' action challenges his society's understandings of status. How do you see concern about status getting in the way of loving action in your community, and what do you do about it?
- Jesus tells his disciples, as Berlin writes, "their whole testimony depends on whether they love others as he loved them." Using this standard, how compelling would you say your congregation's testimony to Christ is? What about your personal witness? What would make these testimonies even more compelling to others?

Matthew 25:34-40

- How do the actions by which the king judges the nations in Jesus' parable help us define the nature of love?
- Why do those who are righteous have no memory of serving the king in the ways he describes? Do you think awareness of serving someone in a loving way diminishes that action's purity? Why or why not?
- Berlin quotes John Wesley as saying we serve the invisible God by serving our neighbors who are "standing visibly before us." What does the king's self-identification with "the least of these who are members of my family" (verse 40) tell us about God's character? What does it tell us about how God calls us to shape our own sense of identity?
- In the rest of Jesus' parable, people who do not lovingly serve the king are consigned to "eternal punishment" (verse 46). What does the king's judgment tell us about how seriously God takes the commandment to love?
- Jesus says the king will judge the nations. How does a nation show love in the ways this parable identifies? How does this parable shape the way you think about your nation's priorities and policies, and about your involvement as a citizen?

Luke 9:23-25

- People sometimes describe their troubles as "my cross to bear." How is that sentiment like or unlike what Jesus is talking about in these verses?
- Why does Jesus specify his followers must take up their crosses daily?
- When, if ever, have you seen someone "gain the whole world" but "lose...themselves" (verse 25)?
- Berlin writes, "We have to let those parts of our nature which are contrary to love die." What must we do or not do to sacrifice those parts of ourselves?
- What practical evidence or signs should we look for to recognize whether and how much we are progressing in our "journey to resurrection" and seeing more of the beauty of our true, God-given identity?

CLOSING THE SESSION

Closing Activity and Prayer (5-10 minutes)

Form pairs of participants. Instruct each pair to sit or stand directly facing each other to play "Mirror." One person in each pair is the leader; the other is the follower. The follower must emulate the leader's facial and body movements as closely and simultaneously as possible. Keep time and, after one minute, instruct participants to switch leader and follower roles. After one more minute, end the game. Ask how the experience of emulating each other in this game is like and unlike emulating Jesus.

Before the closing prayer, thank the group for participating in this study of *Reckless Love*. Invite any closing comments about the study as a whole.

Lead this prayer or one in your own words:

Jesus, you love without limit and command us to do the same. Help us sacrifice all within ourselves that keeps us from living and loving as you intend. May your Spirit transform us ever more fully into your beloved ones, giving glory to God as we love our neighbors and each other. Amen.

Encourage participants to exchange signs and words of peace with each other as they leave.

Extra Activity

Consider arranging a foot-washing service as a way for your group to end its study together. If your congregation is not familiar with foot-washing services, be sure to discuss practical details and expectations in advance (for example: worshipers should come with clean feet and shoes; women should not wear stockings or hose). Enlist your pastor(s) for help planning the service and consult trusted sources online. While foot-washing is not commonly practiced in all Christian traditions and may (and perhaps should) provoke some awkwardness and discomfort, it can still be a powerful expression of humble, serving love.

Emulate Christ

Emulate Christ

Made in the USA
Middletown, DE
16 April 2023

28964108R00038